A gift for:

_____

from:

_____

A Friendship Bouquet

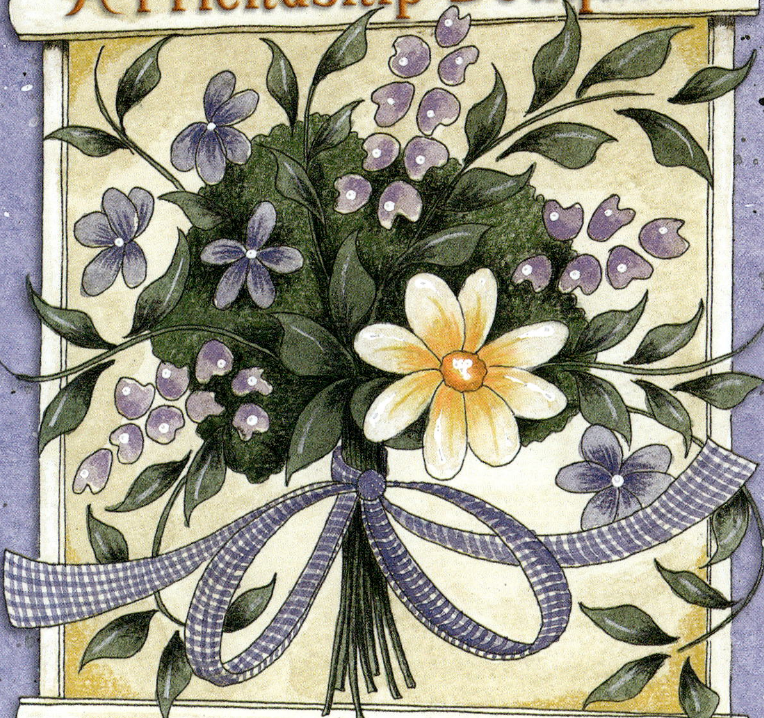

Picked Just for You

Illustrated by Beth Yarbrough

COUNTRYMAN

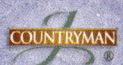

Copyright of text © 2003
by the J. Countryman division of Thomas Nelson Inc.,
Nashville, Tennessee 37214

Copyright of illustrations © 2003 by Beth Yarbrough.
All rights reserved. Represented exclusively by
Linda McDonald, Inc., Charlotte, North Carolina.

Project Manager—Terri Gibbs

All rights reserved. No portion of this publication
may be reproduced, stored in a retrieval system
or transmitted in any form by any means—
electronic, mechanical, photocopying, recording,
or any other—except for brief quotations
in printed reviews, without the prior
written permission of the publisher.

Designed by LeftCoast Design, Portland, Oregon.

ISBN: 14041-0027-X
ISBN: 14041-0085-7

www.thomasnelson.com
www.jcountryman.com

Printed and bound in Italy

This friendly little gift

is meant to

give your heart a lift.

Friendship grows where love goes.

The world
is full of folks,
it's true,
but there is only
one of you.

ANONYMOUS

If dreams were born where gardens grew, and friends were flowers... I'd pick you.

A kind word
is like
a spring day.

YIDDISH PROVERB

You scatter
joy
kindness
laughter

encouragement

sunshine

happiness

good times

wherever you go.

Flowers are the smiles of God's goodness.

—*Wilberforce*

*An act of goodness
is an act of happiness.*

A cheerful
friend is like
a sunny day,
spreading brightness
all along life's way.

Love, consolation,

and peace

bloom only

in the garden

of sweet contentment.

—Martha Anderson

Write down your worries
and cares, pray,
then throw
the paper away.

One of the nicest things you can give another is rapt attention.

I can always
count on you,
to see me through
the ups
and downs
of life.

How I thank God
for the
indescribable gift
of a friend
like you.

You deserve
a hug...
not just today
but every day.

You don't have to be tall to see the moon.

—African Proverb

A heart
full of friendship
is a heart
full of love.

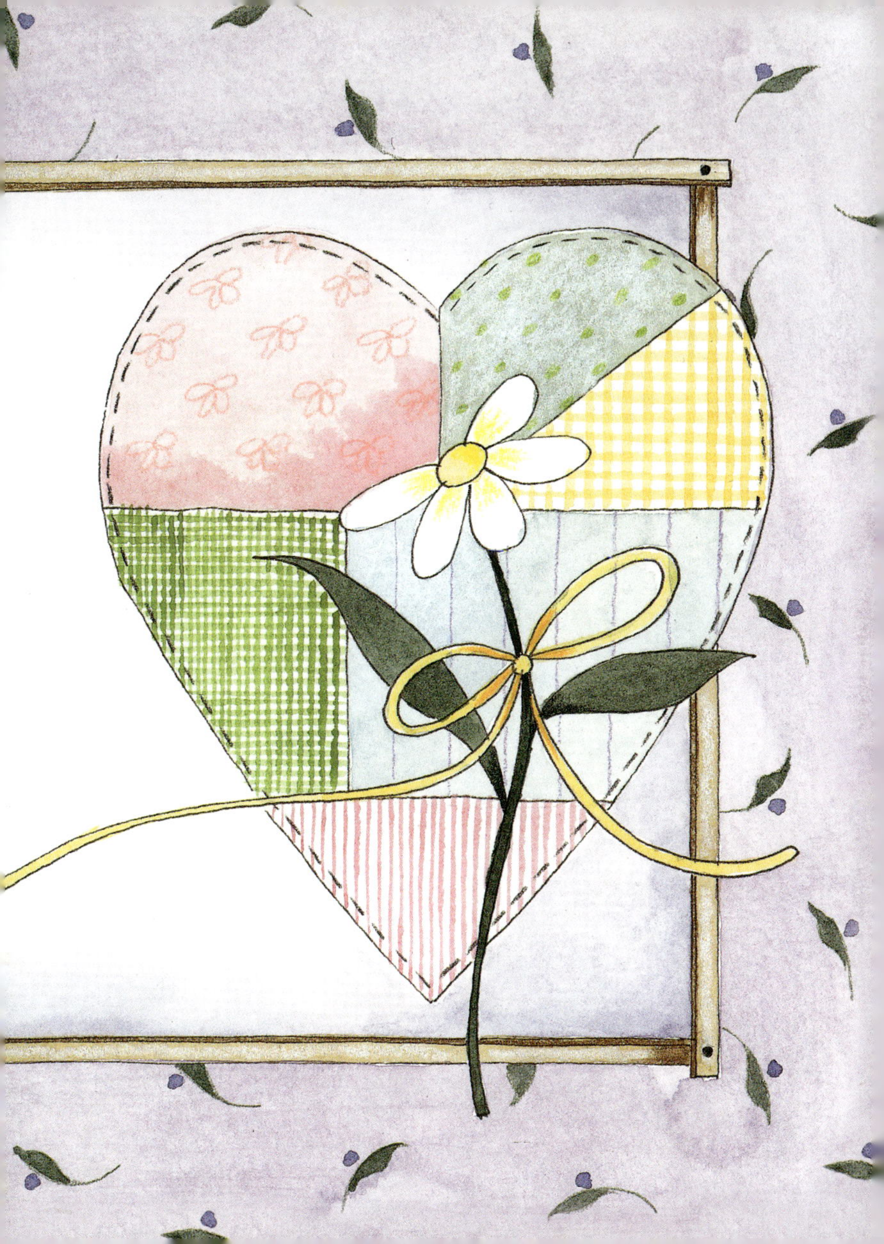

If every good
and kindly deed
formed a flower
in life's sod,

how rich the perfume
and sweet
along the way
to God.

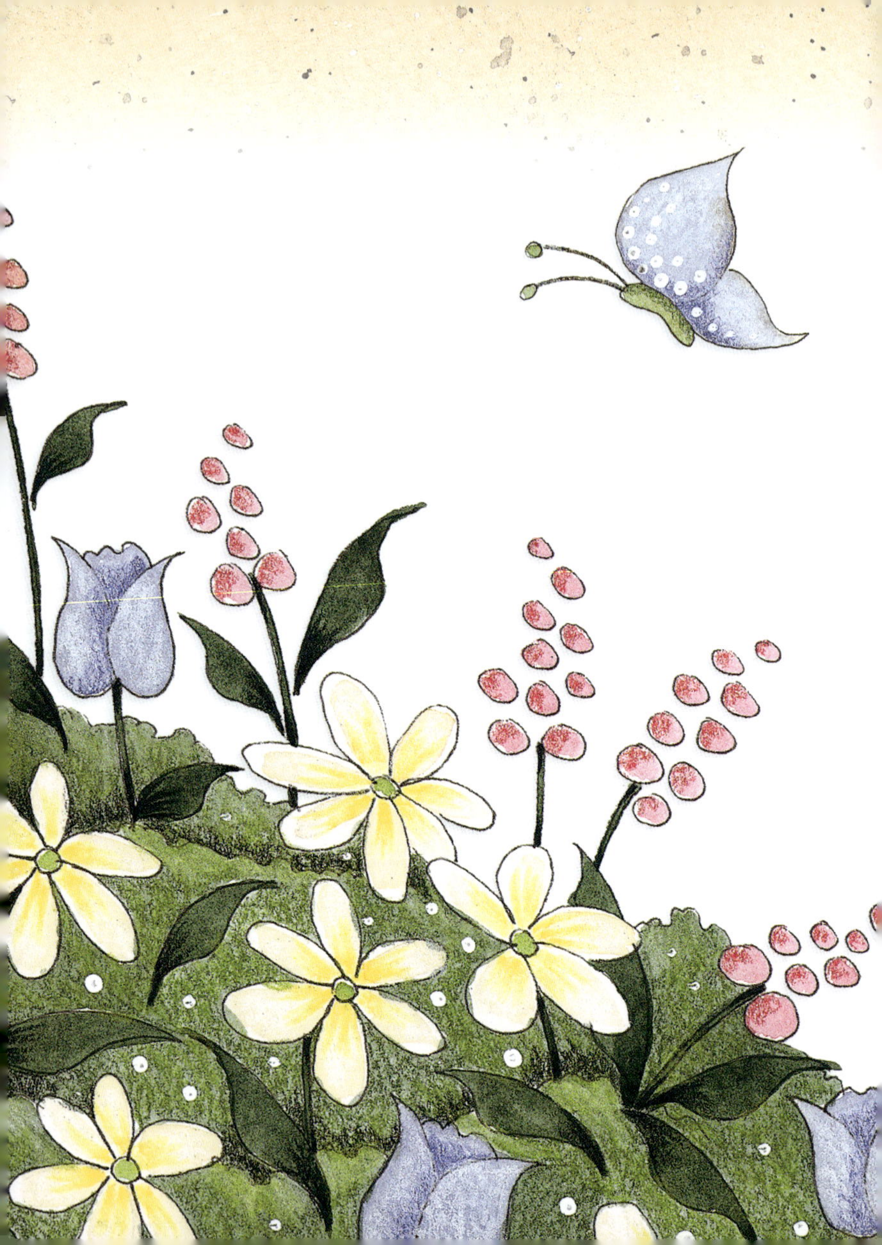

The fun times
may not last,
but true
friendships do.

Friendship

is a gift

from God.

Gratitude can turn

a stranger

into a friend.

—*Yiddish Proverb*

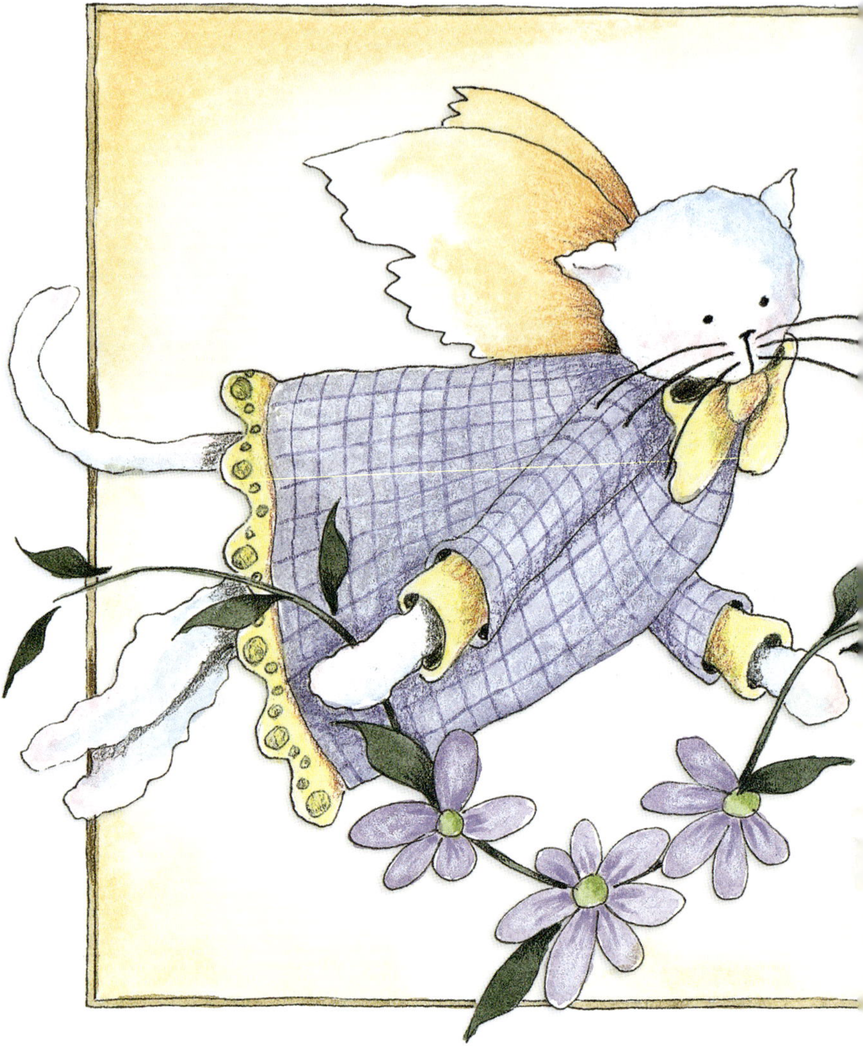

One can
never have
too many flowers...
or friends.

Much of
the happiness in life
depends on
the quality
of your friends.

We must have faith in each other.

—Henry Thoreau

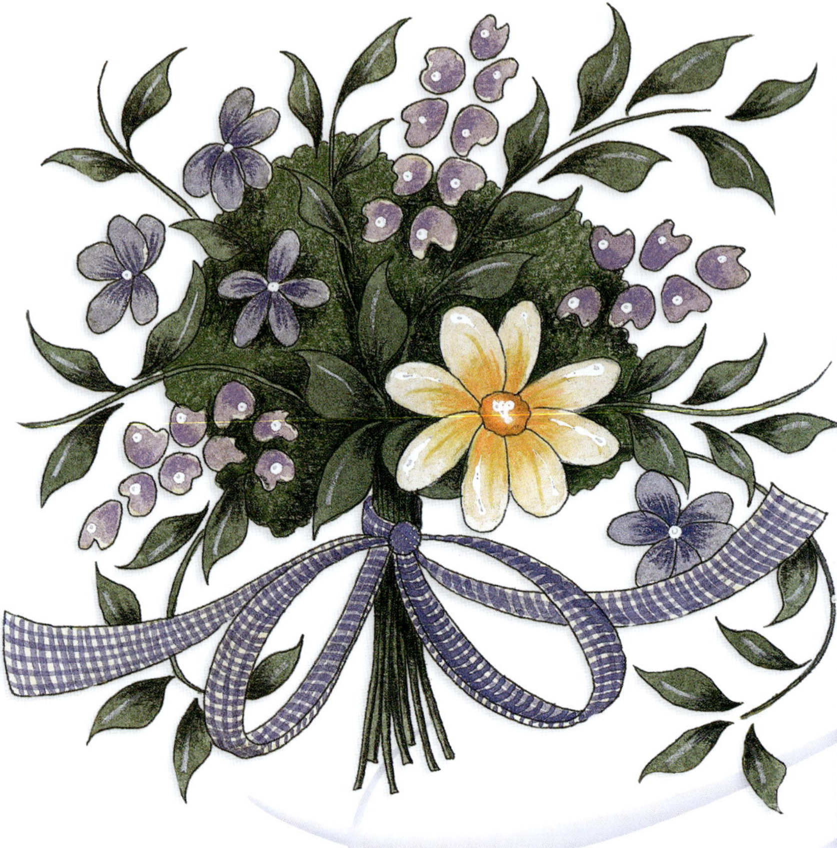

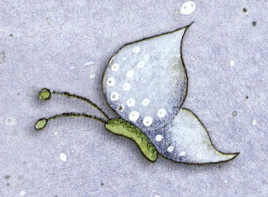

Behind every successful friendship is a substantial amount of coffee and tea.

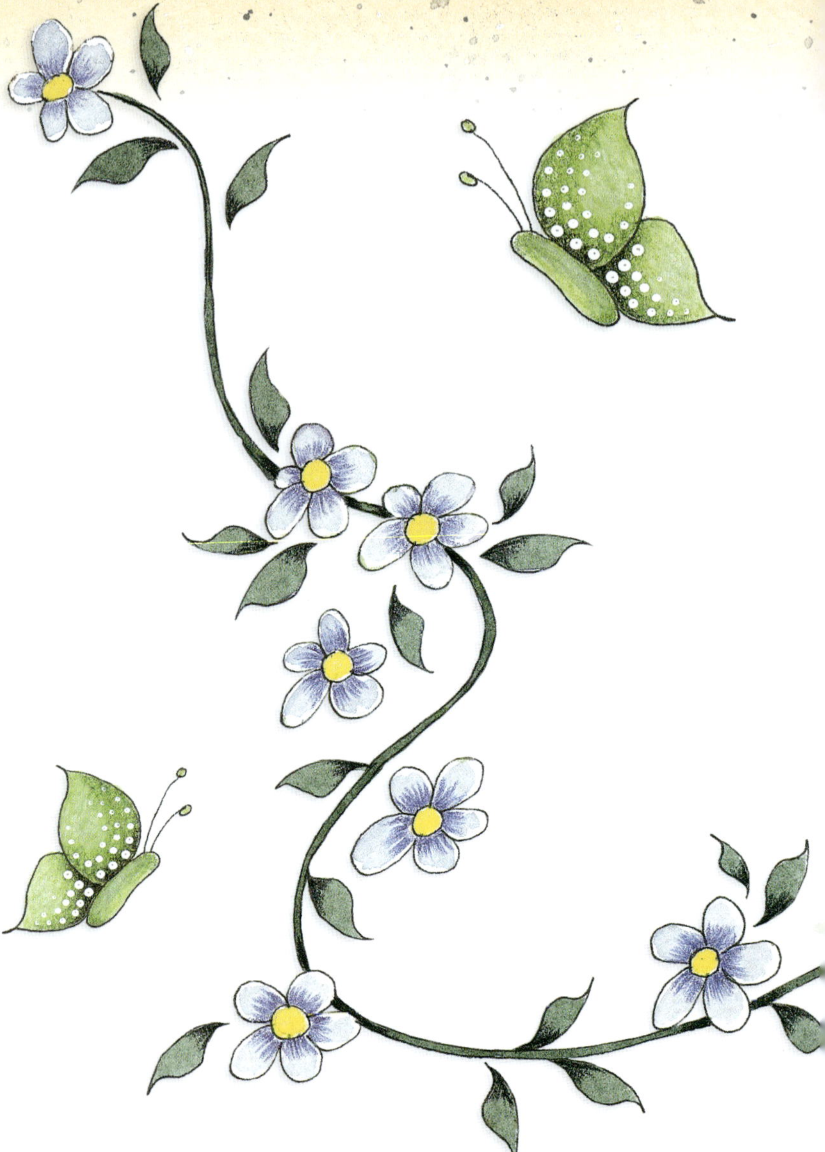

*Reliable friends
who do what they say
are like cool drinks
in sweltering heat—
refreshing!*

—Proverbs 25:10, The Message

What the dew
is to the flower,
gentle words
are to the soul.

—Polly Rupe

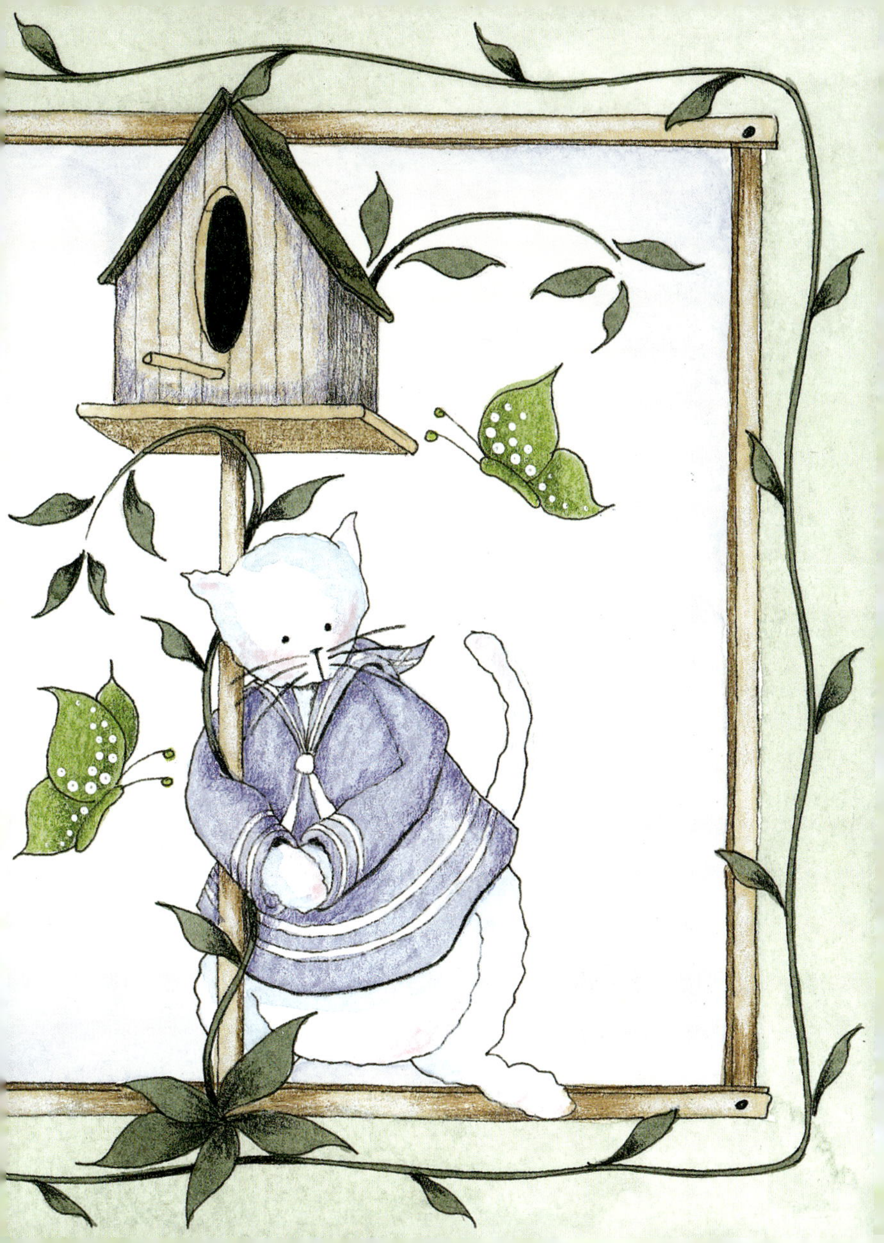